Dedicated with Love

To my children,
who bring sunshine into my life,
and to all the bright little stars
learning their ABCs.

May your journey be filled with
wonder, laughter, and light

Come along with me, let's go A to Z,
To the animal world, wild and free!

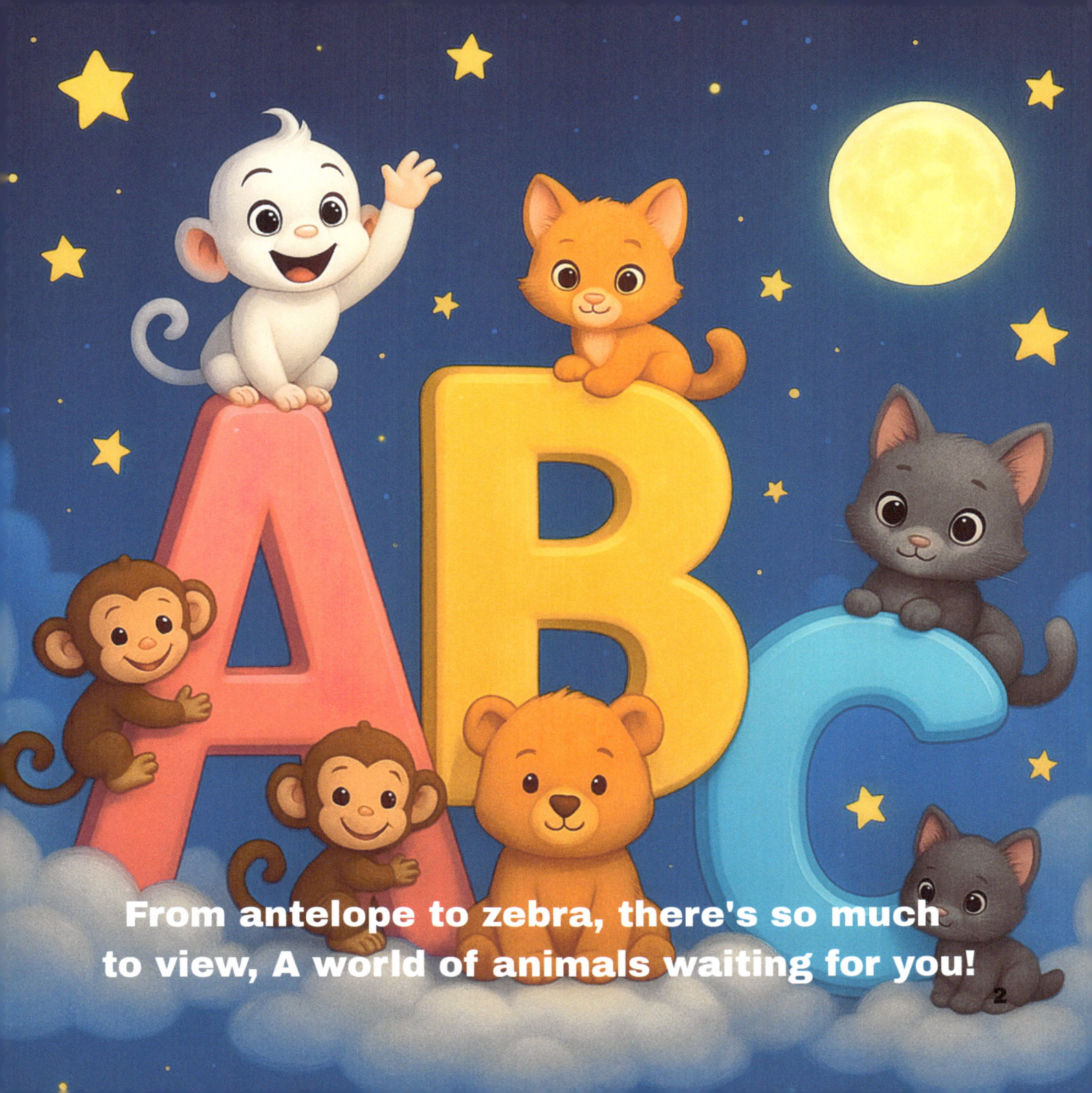

From antelope to zebra, there's so much to view, A world of animals waiting for you!

2

A is for Antelope

3

Antelope

A graceful creature in the wild,
always on the move.

B is for Bear

Bear

A mighty animal with thick fur and a big, strong body.

C is for Cat

Cat

With soft fur and a quiet purr,
always sneaking around.

D is for Dolphin

Dolphin

Gliding gracefully through
the waves of the ocean.

E is for Elephant

Elephant

With its large ears and long trunk,
the giant of the jungle.

F is for Fox

Fox

With its sharp eyes and swift moves,
always on the lookout.

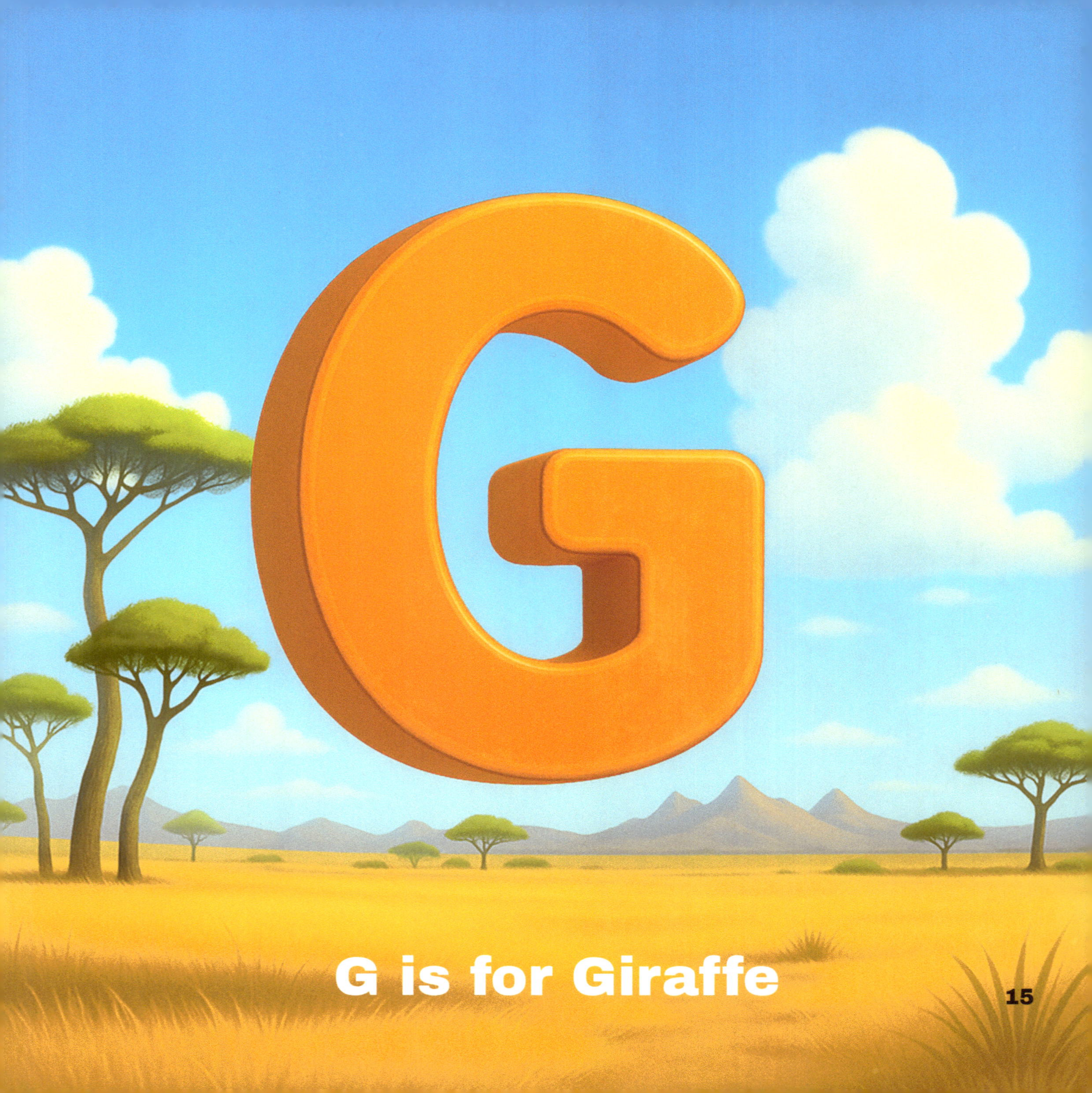

G is for Giraffe

Giraffe

With its long neck reaching
for the treetops.

H is for Horse

Horse

Running with the wind across the open fields.

I is for Iguana

IGUANA

Basking in the warm sunlight,
blending with the leaves.

20

J is for Jaguar

JAGUAR

Stalking through the jungle,
ready to pounce.

K is for Kangaroo

Kangaroo

Hopping across the land with powerful legs.

L is for Lion

LION

A majestic creature with a golden mane, ruling the wild.

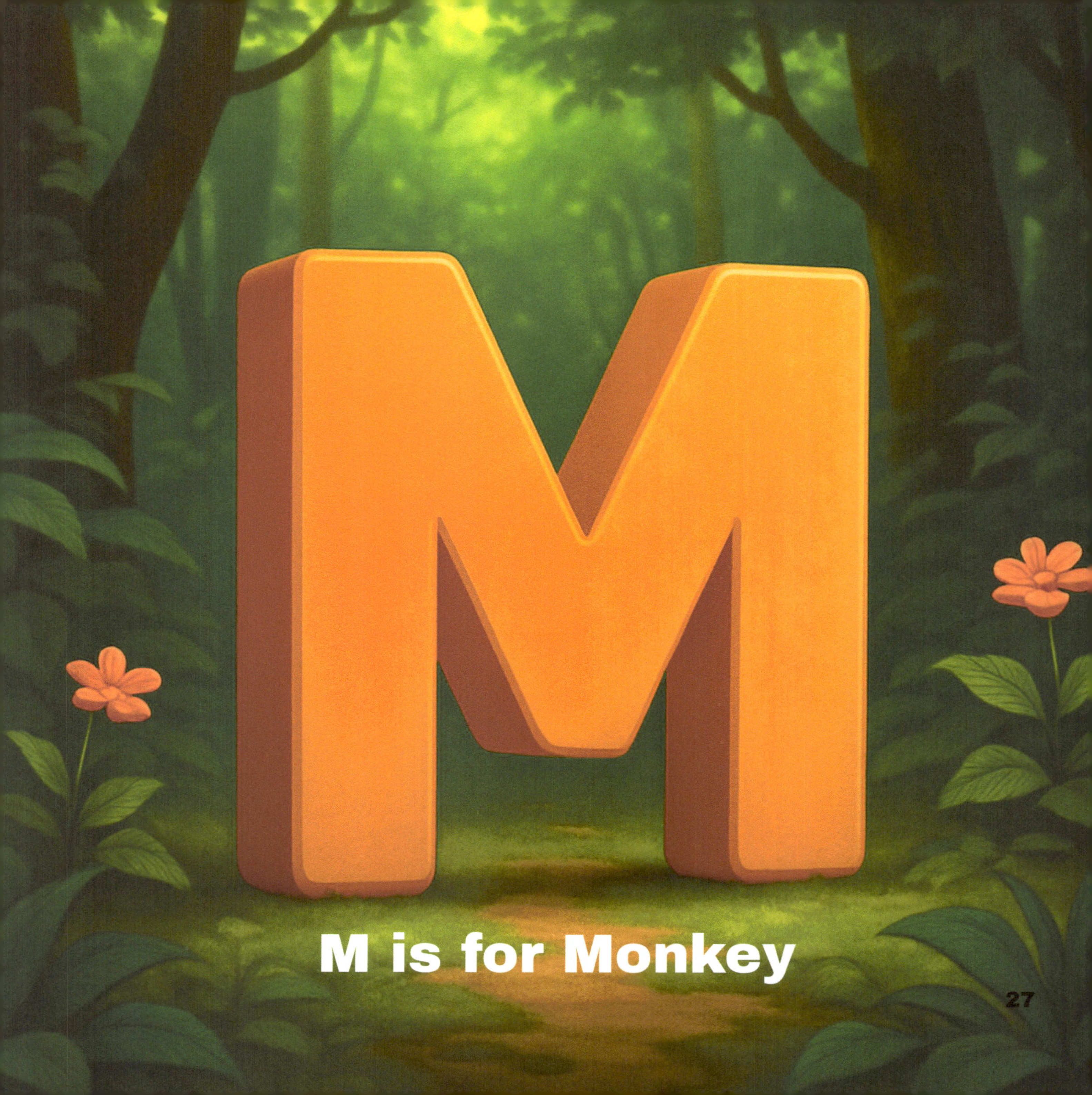

M is for Monkey

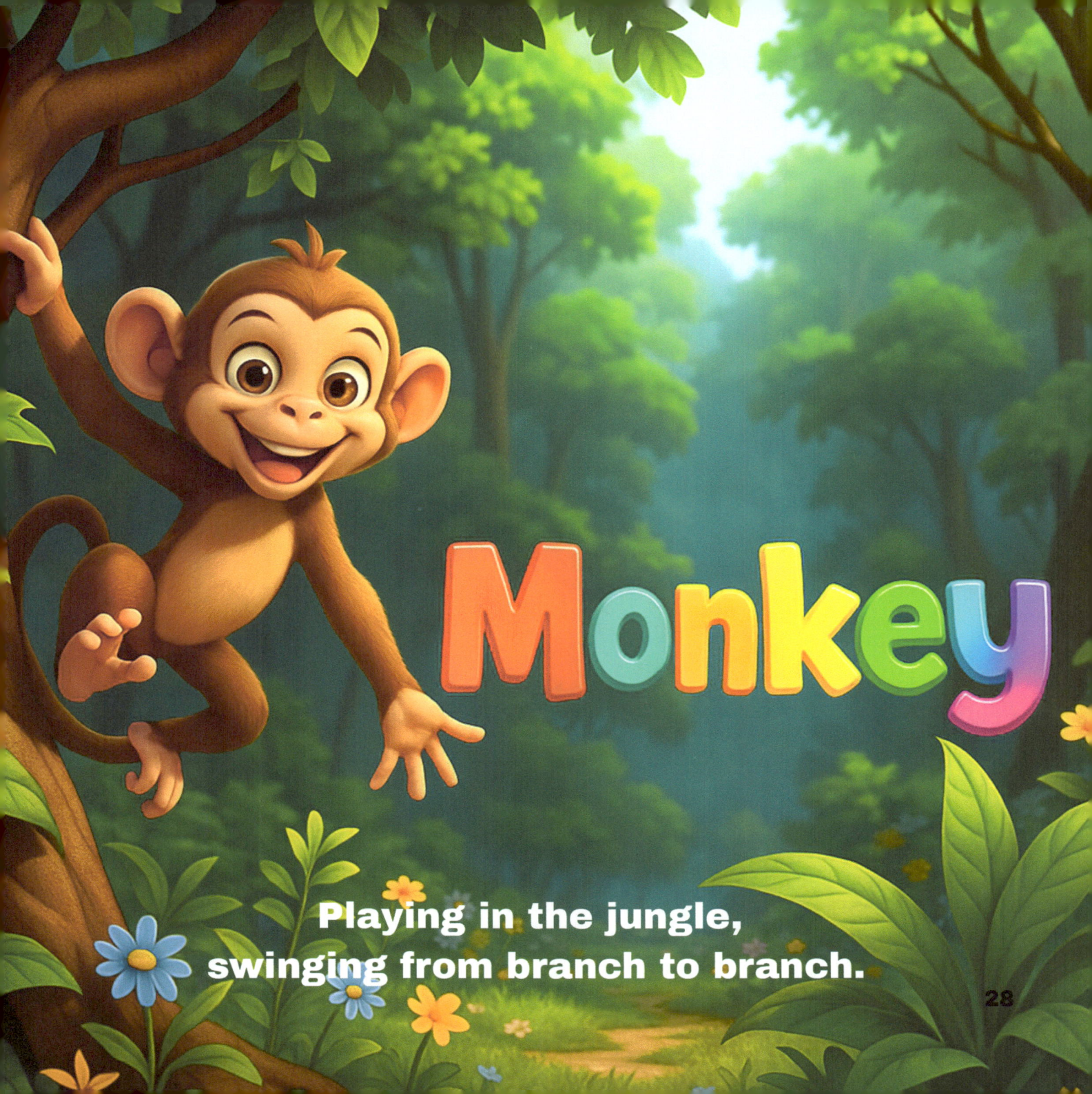

Monkey

Playing in the jungle,
swinging from branch to branch.

N is for Narwhal

Narwhal

The unicorn of the sea,
with a long spiral tusk.

O is for Owl

OWL

With big eyes and soft feathers, watching in the dark.

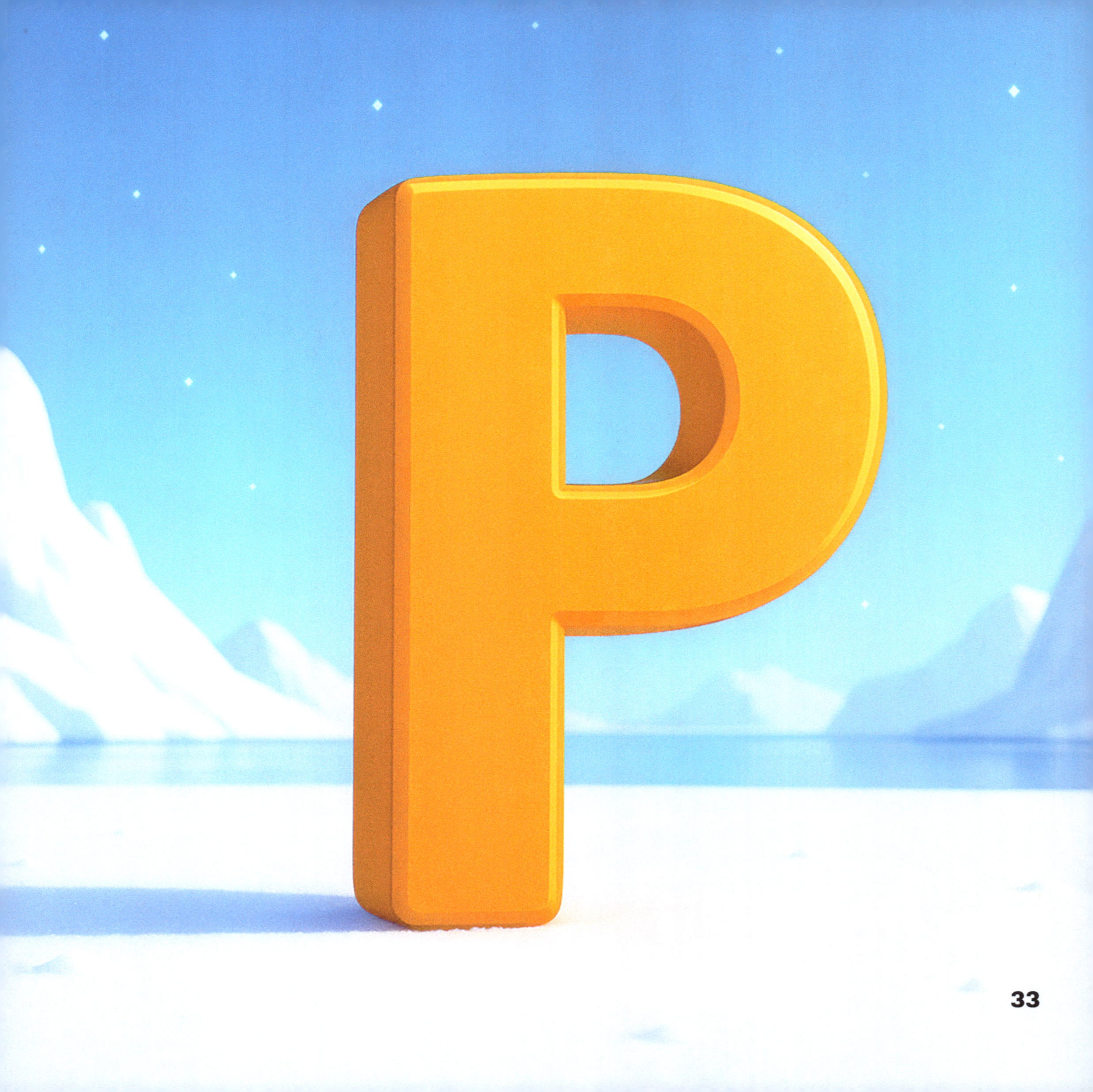
P

Penguin

Siding on the ice and playing in the snow.

Q is for Quail

QUAIL

Darting through the bushes,
always on the go.

R is for Rabbit

Rabbit

Hopping through the meadow, ears twitching.

S is for Snake

SNAKE

Moving silently through
the grass, its scales shimmering.

T is for Tiger

Tiger

A stealthy and powerful predator, moving with grace.

U is for Urchin

43

Urchin

Resting quietly among the coral,
protected by sharp spines.

V is for Vulture

Vulture

Soaring in the sky,
looking for its next meal.

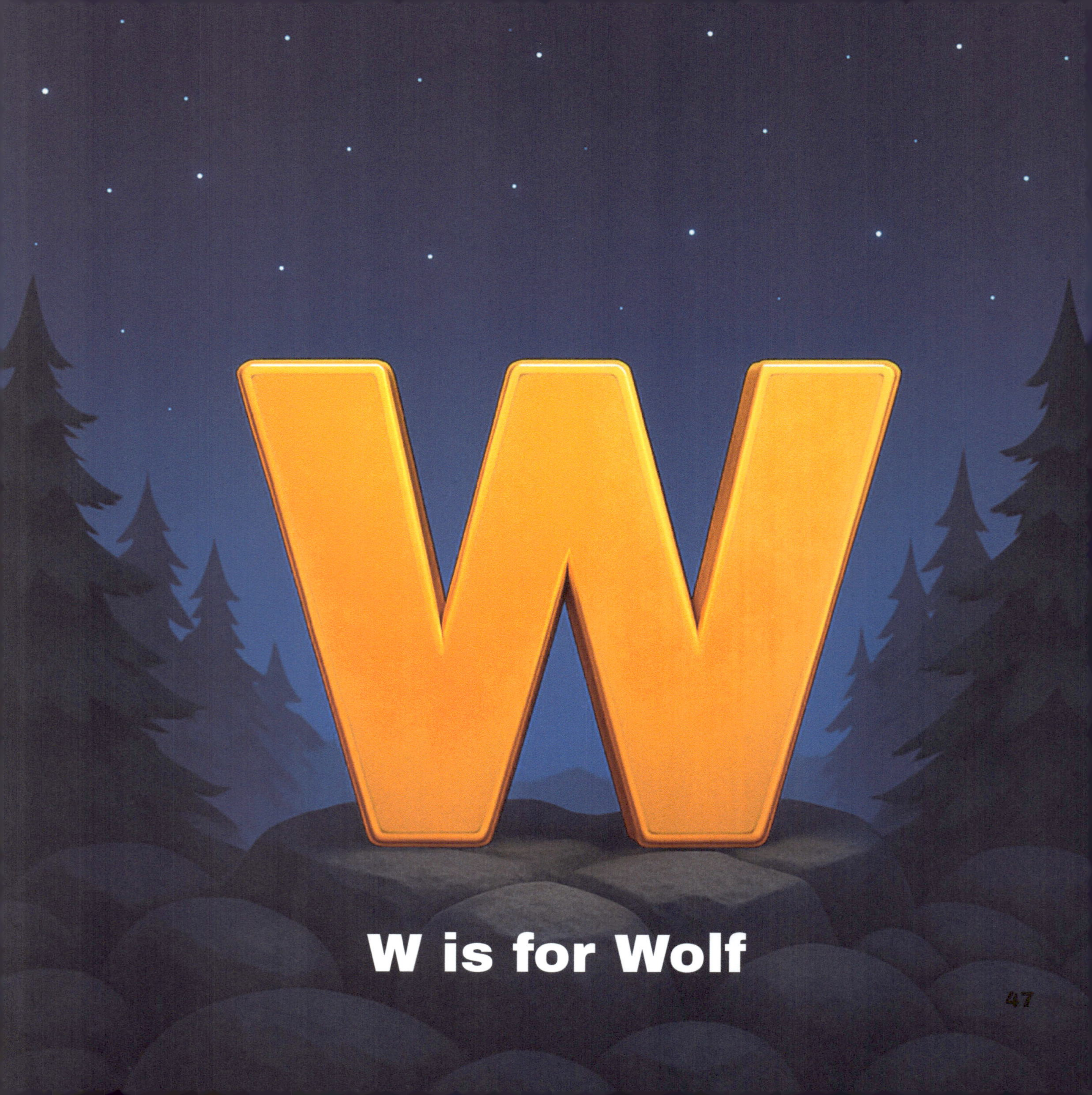

W is for Wolf

Wolf

A wild creature, calling out
to its pack in the night.

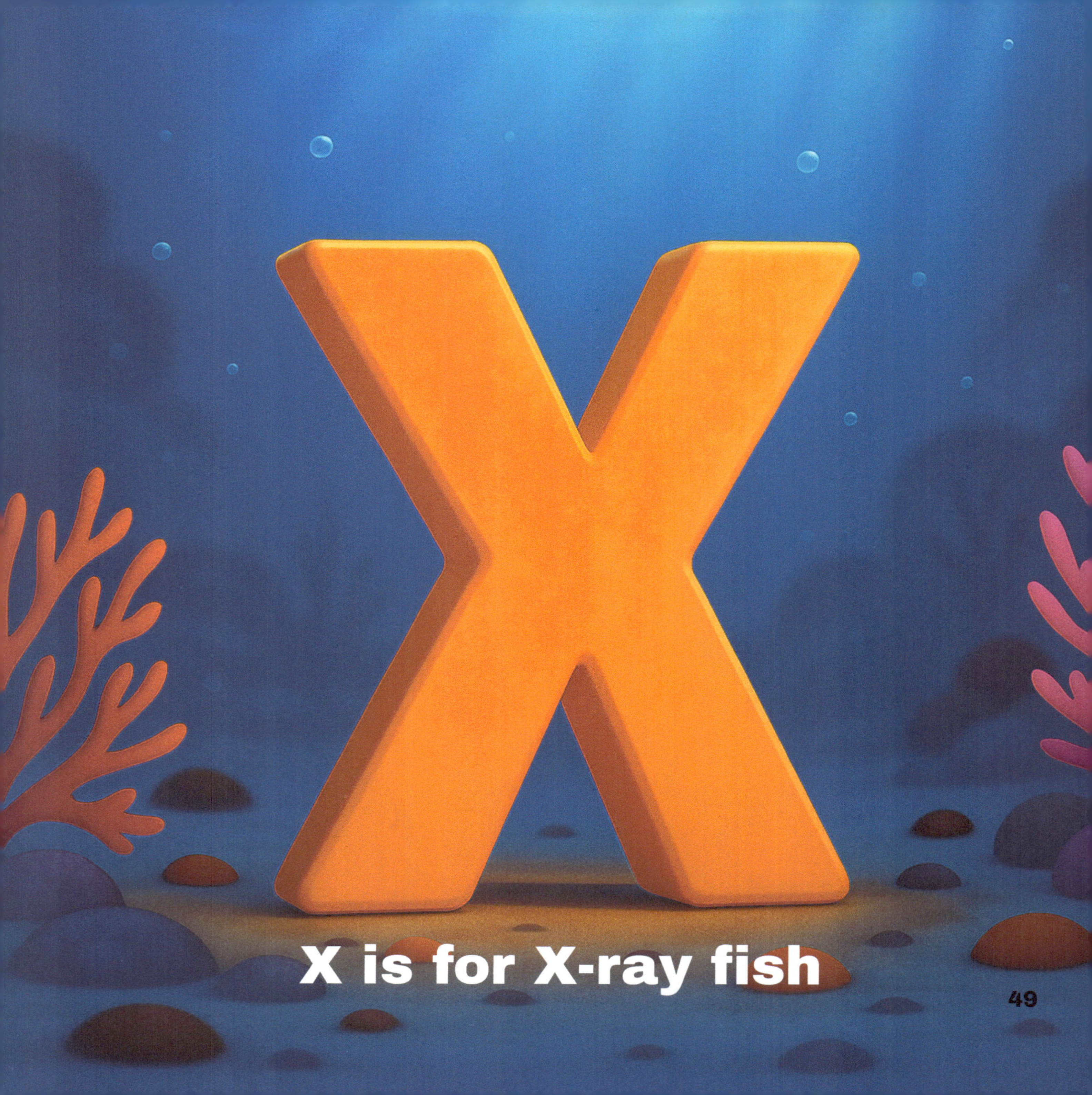

X is for X-ray fish

X-ray

With a transparent body,
swimming through the clear waters.

Y is for Yak

Yak

A sturdy animal with thick fur, climbing high in the mountains.

Z is for Zebra

Zebra

With its unique stripes that help
it blend into the grasslands.

Now you've met them, from A to Z
So many animals wild and free

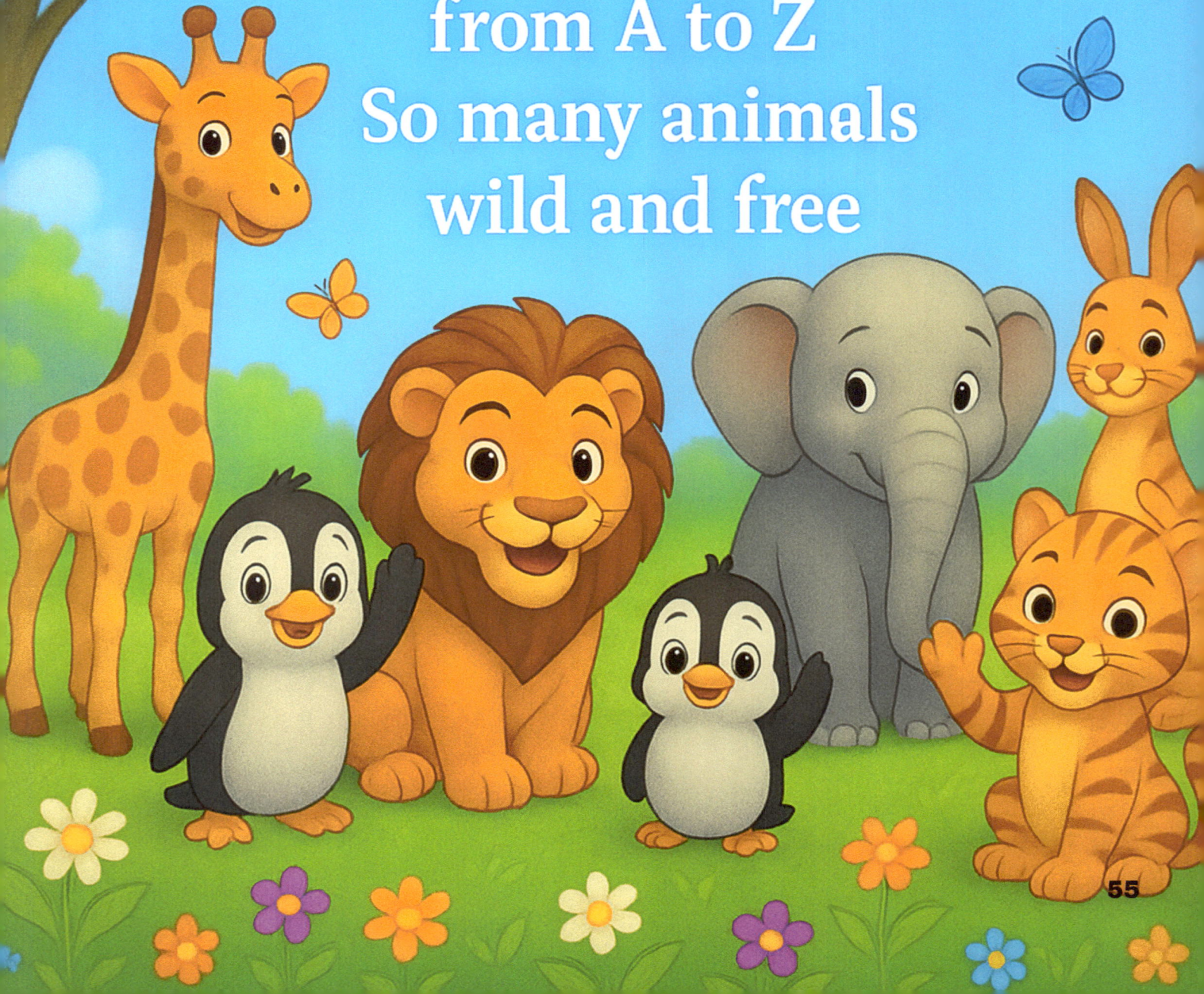

Look through again,
and you will see–
Learning is fun,
as fun can be!

THE END!

www.ingramcontent.com/pod-product-compliance
Lightning Source LLC
LaVergne TN
LVHW072129070426

835513LV00002B/41

9 781967 819027